God-Centered Friendships

Engage in Friendships that Grow and Lift Us Up in Our Faith

Series 1

Sierra Derby
One Ministries Global Inc.

ISBN 978-1-64468-810-6 (Paperback)
ISBN 978-1-64468-811-3 (Digital)

Copyright © 2021 Sierra Derby
All rights reserved
First Edition

All rights reserved. No part of this publication may be reproduced, distributed, or transmitted in any form or by any means, including photocopying, recording, or other electronic or mechanical methods without the prior written permission of the publisher. For permission requests, solicit the publisher via the address below.

Covenant Books, Inc.
11661 Hwy 707
Murrells Inlet, SC 29576
www.covenantbooks.com

To my mom, who set the best example for me while I was growing up. You showed me what being a successful person and, more importantly, a successful Christian truly looked like. Now you have become one of my best friends as an adult.

To my dad, who has always been my best friend. I could always count on you to be there for me no matter what stupid or wise decision I made.

To my husband, the older we get and the longer we're together, the stronger our friendship grows. I'm glad we always work to better our friendship because it betters our marriage.

Contents

Introduction 7

Week 1:   We All Have a Friend in Jesus.....................9

Week 2:   Model Friendship 15

Week 3:   Pray for Each Other 21

Week 4:   Standing Strong Together 25

Week 5:   Daily Talk...30

Week 6:   What Brings You Together? Gossip or God? 35

Week 7:   I Have Your Back 40

Week 8:   Love Trumps Worldly Feelings 45

Additional Note Space...49

Prayer Requests 51

Leading Your Group..53

Introduction

Hello! My name is Sierra Derby, and I am superexcited to be a part of your eight-week study group! I know you will have a ton of fun in your small group and that you will make lots of new friends over the next eight weeks!

This eight-week study of God-Centered Friendships will help you to make, engage in, and keep friendships that are God centered. It will also help you to be more Christlike yourself!

The best way to get the most out of this study series is to engage, truly engage, in the study and be honest with yourself, God, and those around you. God needs us to be honest and insightful; only then will He start His work in us and through us. This study is not about the "blame game." It's about each of us becoming more Christlike in our friendships through self-evaluation. It's important for us to stay balanced! Remember, Satan is a liar and will try to condemn us when we seek God's ways. God doesn't condemn. He graciously convicts us and follows the convictions with teachings and helps for our quest to be Christlike. Let's grow in Him!

The reason I created a study for friendships is I don't think there are enough honest, godly friendships in the world. I don't believe many people today truly understand what a good friendship under God is. We look to Jesus for what He accomplished, but we rarely look to Him to see how His relationships mattered to Him. Relationships are important to God; we'll go through the Old and New Testaments to see how and why. Each week offers questions to dive deeper into each section. There are also some weeks where you can implement what you've learned in a purposeful activity.

Romans 12:5 CEV says, "That's how it is with us. There are many of us, but we each are part of the body of Christ, as well as part of one another."

There are many of us in the body of Christ, and we each have our own important roles for the Kingdom of God. Having Christlike friendships help us to grow into what God originally designed us to be; it also helps build our faith in Christ. We are all important to God, and we should be to each other. God is not a god of scarcity. There is no competition in His kingdom, so there is no need to be any in His Church amongst His children.

I hope you are excited and ready to dive into *God-Centered Friendships Series 1*!

What's in This Study?

In the first week of our study, we will look at two specific encounters Jesus had with people that are not obvious when we think about His relationships in the Bible. Then we look at a friendship that does not involve Jesus directly, but it pleases God because it is centered on His characteristics. As we move through the study, we review Christlike behavior and attitudes to make our friendships successful under God. This study is for the purpose of self-evaluation and growth, friendship evaluation and growth, and of course, growth in our relationship with our Lord Jesus Christ. In the back of this book, there is room for note taking, prayer requests for each week, and leader tips for groups. The verses stated in the study are primarily taken from the CEV and the NIV Bible versions.

Week 1

We All Have a Friend in Jesus

In the Old Testament and the New Testament, we have a friend in Jesus.

Let's visit a couple of areas in both the Old Testament and the New Testament where Jesus shows up as our friend. Don't forget—we still live in the New Testament; the Revelation hasn't happened yet, so everything is very relevant to us today. "Today" is in the New Testament; we live in the times of the Bible!

Old Testament
Hagar, the Runaway

Hagar was an Egyptian woman who became a slave of Sarai, Abram's wife. After many years of waiting on the Lord's promise of Sarai bearing children, she was giving up on her own ability to conceive (assuming that Abram told Sarai about the Lord's promise for her to give up on). So Sarai offered Hagar to Abram for the chance of children.

After Hagar realized she was pregnant, animosity started to develop between the two women. Sarai began treating Hagar unfairly, so Hagar ran away from her master. On Hagar's journey, she stopped at a spring in the desert to rest.

> While she was there, the angel of the Lord [Jesus] came to her and asked, "Hagar, where have you come from, and where are you going?"

She answered, "I'm running away from Sarai, my owner."

The angel said, "Go back to Sarai and be her slave. I will give you a son, who will be called Ishmael, because I have heard your cry for help. And later I will give you so many descendants that no one will be able to count them all. But your son will live far from his relatives; he will be like a wild donkey, fighting everyone, and everyone fighting him."

Hagar thought, "Have I really seen God and lived to tell about it?" So, from then on, she called him, "The God Who Sees Me." (Genesis 16:7–13 CEV)

Hagar had a life she didn't choose. She didn't pick the misfortunes that happened to her. She was pregnant with a child she didn't ask to receive, she had a master that mistreated her because of the master's own wrongdoing, and she was alone and lonely out in the desert going to anywhere but from where she came.

Then out of nowhere, she had an amazing experience! Jesus showed up to her as a friend and as her God, He questioned her to establish personal relationship, He gave her a command I'm sure she wasn't thrilled about, and lastly, He made her a promise for her child. Jesus let her know that He saw her; she wasn't alone, and she didn't have to feel lonely. He was with her, always (Genesis 16:1–16 CEV).

Put yourself in Hagar's place. How do you think Hagar felt about going back to Sarai?

_____

_____

How was Jesus being a friend to Hagar?

Was there a time when God instructed you to go do something even though it wasn't going to be easy?

New Testament
The Samaritan Woman at the Well

Diversity: In the story between Jesus and the Samaritan woman, Jesus has a message to convey to us: we can all be friends no matter the race, national origin, language, class status, or gender. The possibility for two people being friends is dependent on our own desire to be friends (John 4:8–9).

Friends Can Come in Unexpected Places: "Jesus answered, 'You don't know what God wants to give you, and you don't know who is asking you for a drink. If you did, you would ask me for the water that gives life'" (John 4:10 CEV). We can see this previous verse in people that God wants to use in our lives; sometimes the most unsuspecting person could be the person God wants to use for our benefit or the other way around so that we may be used by Him for the benefit of both people involved. Jesus is the life-giving water; you never know whom you might be speaking to when it comes to a stranger. Jesus was the Samaritan's woman greatest friend because He was telling her about eternal life!

Lifting Her Up with Faith: After the Samaritan woman questioned Jesus's previous answer with skepticism, He lifted her up in faith explaining how she could have eternal life with the true life-giving water. "Jesus answered, 'Everyone who drinks this water will get thirsty again. But no one who drinks the water I give will ever be thirsty again. The water I give will become in that person a flowing fountain that gives eternal life.' The woman replied, 'Sir, please give me a drink of that water! Then I won't get thirsty and have to come to this well again'" (John 4:13–15 CEV).

Jesus was such a good friend to her who came from an unexpected place. In the end, Jesus revealed to her that certain parts of her life were not right, but He didn't love her any less. Because of His love and ability to speak life into her, she put her faith in Him and then went and told many others about Him (John 4:1–42).

What enables us to want to be friends?

_____

_____

The least expected person could turn out to be the very person God wants you to be friends with. Do you have an open mind to be friends with whomever God brings to you?

_____

_____

How can you lift someone up in faith?

_____

_____

Allowing Jesus to purify our hearts allows room for what God wants to put in our lives. If our heart is full of bitterness and hate, there isn't room for love and joy. If our hearts are filled with ourselves, instead of Jesus, then our hearts don't have room for others. When Jesus takes residency in our heart, there is more room in it than ever before for others to come in as well.

Each of us should please our neighbors for
their good, to build them up. For even Christ

did not please himself but, as it is written: "The insults of those who insult you have fallen on me." For everything that was written in the past was written to teach us, so that through the endurance taught in the Scriptures and the encouragement they provide we might have hope. May the God who gives endurance and encouragement give you the same attitude of mind toward each other that Christ Jesus had, so that with one mind and one voice you may glorify the God and Father of our Lord Jesus Christ. Accept one another, then, just as Christ accepted you, in order to bring praise to God. (Romans 15:2–7 NIV)

Discuss amongst the group what having Jesus in your heart is like. How has your heart been opened since Jesus came in?

If you haven't accepted Jesus into your heart, you can let your group leader know, and they can help you with accepting Him into your heart, or you can do this in your personal time with God.

Here is a prayer to ask Him into your heart:

Jesus, I believe you are the Son of God, who died on the cross to cover my sins with your blood, to restore me to the Father. Today, I choose to turn from my sins and every part of my life that does not please you. I ask you to come into my heart as I give myself to you. I receive your forgiveness and ask you to fill me with your love, to take your rightful place in my life as my Savior and Lord. Thank you, God. In Jesus's name, I pray. Amen.

Congratulations on becoming a child of Christ! Ask your group members to pray for you, as this is the most important step in your life. Welcome to the kingdom!

Praying for each other is one way to help others tear down personal walls and gain new friendships!

Allow the leader of the small group to pray. This is a great time to share prayer requests. After prayer requests are shared, this is also a good time to share if God has been meeting the previous week's prayer requests of each member. Expressing His works is a great way for driving faith. If you don't see Him working yet for a specific prayer request, don't be afraid to open discussion. Small groups are considered a "safe zone" that is condemnation-free.

Please remember that prayer requests are sacred and are not to be used as gossip outside the group. Respect each member of the small group, and take to heart their needs for this week.

Week 2

Model Friendship

The Relationship between King David and Jonathan

The friendship between King David and Jonathan represents a Christlike friendship: *selflessness, love,* and *loyalty.*

"Jonathan thought as much of David as he did himself" (1 Samuel 18:1 CEV).

When David and Jonathan became friends, Jonathan quickly admired David and thought as much of his friend as he did himself. They immediately started building a friendship based on selflessness by "loving your neighbor more than yourself" (Mark 12:31).

When Jesus came to earth, His character modeled selfless love for us. He continues to model this because that's naturally who He is. Although this is Christ's natural trait, we must work at selfless love. Fortunately, we have God to help us!

Love creates a selfless attitude in us when we love others like God loves us. Search within yourself, and answer the following questions honestly. The questions are for personal growth opportunities. If you need help answering the questions, don't be afraid to ask God for insight.

Do you think you love others more than yourself?

_____

_____

Who can you show love to this week?

_____

_____

What is something you can do to show love to someone else?

_____

_____

How will this improve your selfless behavior as a servant in Christ's body?

_____

_____

Love isn't just an action (a selfless behavior), it is also a transformation in the heart. Our hearts open when Jesus comes in and transforms it from wicked to holy. We go from loving few to wanting and being able to love many.

Early on in their friendship, David and Jonathan promised each other with a commitment to be always loyal in their friendship (1 Samuel 18:3). Loyalty offers a lot in friendship; loyalty acts as a way of support and dedication toward someone else. Loyalty is the counterpart to selfless behavior. As we see between the friendship of David and Jonathan, loyalty was the second thing to be modeled by the two men.

What does loyalty mean to you?

_____

_____

How is Jesus loyal to you?

_____

_____

Loyalty is a lasting commitment. Can people count on you to be loyal?

_____

_____

Jonathan helped David be successful in the eyes of King Saul. Jonathan gave David many of his own things. He stood with David and offered support during David's time of success (1 Samuel 18:4). Many times, we become jealous of another's success, especially when we are in a "dry season." God has more to offer us other than worthless dry seasons when we look to Him. He uses every moment, including dry seasons, for a purpose.

Sinful jealousy is not God's way. "You are still worldly. For since there is jealousy and quarreling among you, are you not worldly? Are you not acting like mere humans" (1 Corinthians 3:3 NIV)? Jonathan did not allow any jealousy in his heart when it came to David, no matter the amount of success David gained. Jonathan was right there by David's side.

Imagine how easy jealousy could have snuck into Jonathan's heart against David. First, King Saul was Jonathan's own father. Therefore, Jonathan should have become king following Saul. Yet David—a mere farmer's son, an outsider to Jonathan's family—was going to be taking the position as king (1 Samuel 16:1–13). God was prepping David for the king position as His Spirit was with him. David was good at everything he did because God was with him. People chanted for David when returning from wars (1 Samuel 18:7). Although, the chanting was for David and not against Jonathan, it was against Jonathan's father. We can see how easily Jonathan could have become jealous of David.

When sin entered mankind's heart, it caused us to start comparing ourselves to others. We look at how well others are doing, and it gives us the idea that scarcity is a factor in the Kingdom of God. We think that God isn't capable of making all our lives rich. We become jealous, judgmental, and depressed when we see someone close to us "doing better" than us. However, God looks at His creation and purposes differently than we do. We think "rich" is purely monetary and possessions, but God sees "rich" in all aspects, primarily characteristic. Since our view of an abundant life is limited to earthly things, our minds start on a downward spiral of fear, jealousy, and doubt thinking that God doesn't have a plan specifically laid out for each one of us. But I assure you, He does!

We all go through highs and lows in life. We are blessed to walk in all seasons with those close to us, as we "Rejoice with those who rejoice; mourn with those who mourn" (Romans 12:15 NIV).

It's detrimental when we compare ourselves to those around us. We either think we aren't keeping up and doing enough, or we think we are better than those who aren't keeping up with us. Either way, it's prideful and keeps our focus away from God and His kingdom. Part of having a Christlike friendship is being able to depend on one another through all seasons of life with exhibiting trust and care for the other person.

Selflessness, love, and loyalty go hand in hand. It allows our eyes to be opened and see God's ways, His expectations, and the bigger picture for all of us. We see that it doesn't just involve one of us but all of us.

In what ways can you support your friend(s)?

In what ways can we help each other combat against the downward spiral of fear, jealousy, and doubt?

GOD-CENTERED FRIENDSHIPS

Dry seasons are not a form of scarcity in the kingdom. What are dry seasons in our faith for?

_____

_____

David and Jonathan displayed to us what it is like to have a friendship built on God's foundation. Just like they modeled a Christlike friendship for us, we can model a Christlike friendship for others. God experiences great joy when we connect with others and not act like those of this world. He places people in our lives for our benefit but also for His glory. Having a God-centered friendship models to the world how good He is.

Do you believe that God has a perfectly laid plan for each one of us?

_____

_____

What are some ways you can connect this week with those in your small group?

_____

_____

As a group, discuss King David's and Jonathan's friendship. What stands out to you as admirable characteristics?

_____

_____

Praying for each other is one thing that you can do for others to express selflessness, love, and loyalty.

Allow the leader of the small group to pray. Then this is a great time to share prayer requests. After prayer requests are shared, this is also a good time to share if God has been meeting the previous week's prayer requests of each member. Expressing His works is a great way for driving faith. If you don't see Him working yet for a specific prayer request, don't be afraid to open discussion. Small groups are considered a "safe zone" that is condemnation-free.

Please remember that prayer requests are sacred and are not to be used as gossip outside the group. Respect each member of the small group and take to heart their needs for this week.

Week 3

Pray for Each Other

Jesus Prayed with and for Others

"But I have prayed for you, that your faith may not fail; and you, when once you have turned again, strengthen your brothers" (Luke 22:32 NASB).

Jesus is always praying for us, even now in heaven. "Who then is the one who condemns? No one. Christ Jesus who died—more than that, who was raised to life—is at the right hand of God and is also interceding for us" (Romans 8:34 NIV).

He knows we are not strong enough on our own, for we need others to pray with us and for us. Jesus prayed for Peter before Jesus went to the cross. Jesus knew Peter was not strong enough on his own. Therefore, Jesus prayed, "Simon, Simon, Satan has asked to sift all of you like wheat. But I have prayed for you, Simon, that your faith will not fail. And when you have turned back, strengthen your brothers" (Luke 22:31–32 NIV).

Satan asks to sift us just as he asked to sift Peter. This was not the first and only time in the Bible where God shows us that Satan has such requests. For example, Satan did the same thing to Job (Job 1:9–12). While Satan was causing chaos in Job's life, Job needed friends who would pray for him to get through his troubles with strength.

Job did have friends, but his friends didn't pray for him. Instead, they lectured him, talking to him like they knew what was going on in Job's life and why it was happening, but they didn't know. Job would have benefited much more from friends who just prayed. Job did make it through the hard times, eventually. However, Job prayed for his friends; because he did this, he saved his friends from God's wrath. God was angry with Job's friends, for what they said of God was not true (Job 42:8). God lectured Job's friends and then Job. Fortunately, God is gracious.

What does it mean to you that Jesus is praying for you right now and always?

_____

_____

Why did Jesus pray for Peter before Jesus went to the cross?

_____

_____

Do you think Job would have benefited more if his friends prayed for him instead of lecturing him about his life?

_____

_____

It is a humbling experience for both parties when we pray for each other. "Do nothing from selfishness or empty conceit, but with humility of mind regard one another as more important than yourselves; do not merely look out for your own personal interests, but also for the interests of others" (Philippians 2:3–4 NASB).

We need righteous friends to stand in the gap for us without casting judgment. We need someone who can be there for us during the good times so we don't become too full of ourselves and during the bad times to petition for strength and courage for us when we don't feel adequate.

James states, "Therefore, confess your sins to one another and pray for one another, that you may be healed. The prayer of a righ-

GOD-CENTERED FRIENDSHIPS

teous person has great power as it is working" (James 5:16 ESV). When we confess our sins to those who are righteous, they can pray for our guidance and renewal in Christ.

When James says, "That you may be healed," he isn't necessarily talking about a physical ailment. He is talking about a sinful heart. When we pray for others to overcome their sin, we are praying for their healing.

Why do we always need to be praying for our friends?

_____

_____

Why should we confess our sins to someone we trust?

_____

_____

Why do we need to be healed of our sinful heart?

_____

_____

Christlike friends can call down the kingdom of heaven on you. They can also work with you on strengthening your prayer life. Jesus prayed with his friends, and He prayed for His friends (John 17). Praying friends can do just like Jesus did! Asking God for His will to be done is crucial for yourself and for your friends.

How can you strengthen your prayer life with Christ and friends?

_____

_____

Practice praying with your small group friends now! The leader should start the group in prayer, and then each member (if feeling comfortable to do so) takes their own turn saying a short prayer to add on. If you feel the group is too large for this exercise, split the group into smaller groups.

After spending time in prayer with each other, discuss how you could add this into your daily life outside of group and church and how you think this will be beneficial to your friends and to you.

Implement the Study!

Assign accountability partners this week for friendship prayer! Check in throughout the week. Let your accountability partner know how you're doing with your friendship prayer. Ask them if they have noticed a positive impact in their life, or you can pray together.

Praying for each other is one way to get closer to your friends and to God!

Allow the leader of the small group to pray. Then this is a great time to share prayer requests. After prayer requests are shared, this is also a good time to share if God has been meeting the previous week's prayer requests of each member. Expressing His works is a great way for driving faith. If you don't see Him working yet for a specific prayer request, don't be afraid to open discussion. Small groups are considered a "safe zone" that is condemnation-free.

Please remember that prayer requests are sacred and are not to be used as gossip outside the group. Respect each member of the small group and take to heart their needs for this week.

Week 4

Standing Strong Together

Stand Strong. Stand Together. Stand in the Name of Jesus.

> My prayer is not for them alone. I pray also for those who will believe in me through their message, that all of them may be one, Father, just as you are in me and I am in you. May they also be in us so that the world may believe that you have sent me. I have given them the glory that you gave me, that they may be one as we are one—I in them and you in me—so that they may be brought to complete unity. Then the world will know that you sent me and have loved them even as you have loved me. (John 17: 20–23 NIV)

Having someone to stand with makes our lonely feelings go away, even if it's only for a moment. That moment someone takes time out of their day to comfort us can be day changing, season changing, or life changing. We are created to be in community with others. When we don't have someone to lean on in the good and bad times, it is natural that we feel completely alone.

We are never alone with Jesus, because He is always by our side and in our heart. Jesus is our most comforting partner we can have in any situation. He gives what no one else can. However, Jesus will use others to speak into us. There are times that we listen better to a physical source rather than an internal source. It may be more clarifying to us at the time, or it may catch our attention easier.

"If you feel left alone in an unknown place, remember the Lord is on His throne" (Marissa Henley).

Who has God used in your life recently to express comfort toward a situation?

_____

_____

Be open. Be ready. Are you ready to be used by God?

_____

_____

How has Jesus been there for you when no one else was?

_____

_____

God created us to be together in all forms of relationships. Therefore, it makes sense that the enemy, Satan, wants to keep us separated and secluded. When the devil can get us isolated and make us feel alone, he can start a mental war on us. He uses our loneliness and our aloneness to his advantage. You're always weaker in battle when you stand alone. We need Christlike people around to help us stand strong against the enemy. Therefore, Christian friendships are crucial in life.

"Some friends don't help, but a true friend is closer than family" (Proverbs 18:24 CEV). We lean on our friends for support, prayer, and advice. Those in the body of Christ are there to help us stand strong against the enemy and normal, everyday struggles. The best kind of friend is one that we can turn to in the physical presence at a moment's notice, someone to whom we are comfortable with and look up.

GOD-CENTERED FRIENDSHIPS

How can you fight against the enemy's mental war on you?

_____

_____

Why are Christlike friends important in your life?

_____

_____

How can you tell the difference between enemy warfare and normal, everyday struggles?

_____

_____

One of the enemy's tools for creating isolation is social media. It may appear that we have a ton of friends to help us stand strong, but do we? God created us to be in close relationships. He didn't intend for us to hide behind a technological screen. Social media implies that we have community, and it satisfies every part of our being short term—*except* our heart. Close communion with others, face-to-face, allows us to celebrate and mourn together intimately (Romans 12:15).

We don't need to have two hundred or one thousand "friends" as social media suggests. We need one or two that we call upon to help us stand strong in the name of Jesus. Luke 5:17–39 tells us the story of a man who had committed, persistent friends who were willing to lift him up on the roof, remove roofing tiles, and lower him down to see Jesus. They did this so he could be healed. It was the only way, and they knew it. Wow! He had friends he could count on and stand strong with. He wouldn't have these friends from any kind of social media site.

What did the crippled man's friends have to sacrifice so they could get him to Jesus?

_____

_____

Do you think his acquaintances would have done the same thing for him?

_____

_____

Do you believe that social media can be used by the enemy to keep us isolated from experiencing true intimate friendships?

_____

_____

A friend to stand strong with only comes from creating a personal, heartfelt relationship in the flesh. We can't let the enemy isolate us; we need friends like the crippled man had in Luke for our everyday life.

With whom do you stand strong?

_____

_____

How can you get stronger together?

_____

_____

GOD-CENTERED FRIENDSHIPS

Jesus will always stand strong with you. What are some ways that He stands strong for you?

_____

_____

Praying for each other is one way to stand strong with friends—for any day of life.

Allow the leader of the small group to pray. Then this is a great time to share prayer requests. After prayer requests are shared, this is also a good time to share if God has been meeting the previous week's prayer requests of each member. Expressing His works is a great way for driving faith. If you don't see Him working yet for a specific prayer request, don't be afraid to start a discussion. Small groups are considered a "safe zone" that is condemnation-free.

Please remember that prayer requests are sacred and are not to be used as gossip outside the group. Respect each member of the small group and take to heart their needs for this week.

Week 5

Daily Talk

We Speak Words Out of Our Mouth Every Day

and We Are Responsible for What Comes Out

"So then, each of us will give an account of ourselves to God" (Romans 14:12 NIV).

We all have "daily talk" with someone, whether it is with family, coworkers, or friends. The question becomes, what do we talk about? Is Scripture involved? Do our conversations predominantly revolve around others? Do we like to talk about ourselves the most?

Take a minute to analyze recent conversations you've had with those around you to answer the previous paragraph questions. You may discuss this with the group and collaborate how you could have steered some conversations differently.

Ephesians 4:29 CEV says to "stop all our dirty talk. Say the right thing at the right time and help others by what you say." This means to be led by the Holy Spirit to ensure what comes from our mouth is coming from God (Luke 12:12). The key to a healthy conversation is having it well balanced between two or more people and bringing it back to God, if possible. This can grow our faith in ways that we cannot achieve on our own.

So what is "dirty talk"? Dirty talk is anything that is not pleasing or acceptable to God. God created all topics to talk about and all emotions to feel because He created all things. However, sin has caused us to turn all topics and emotions from holy to dirty when sin entered our hearts. For example, sexual talk isn't bad when it is with your spouse or when it is in the form of psychological or educational, but Satan has taken the topic of sex and turned it dirty and away from God. We forget that the origin of all things comes from God, but all things have become twisted by evil.

"What comes out of the mouth reveals what is in the heart."

What do you talk about most with those close to you?

_____

_____

How can you stop the "dirty talk" and start purifying your words?

_____

_____

Do you consider the dirty, senseless talk as sin?

_____

_____

There are many verses throughout the Bible that explain the importance of what our mouths, tongues, and words do to ourselves and to those around us. Paul tells us to stop the dirty, senseless talk. Therefore, if it is not going to help anyone or be of benefit, there is no point saying it. The Holy Spirit will guide our conversations with others if we choose to listen to Him. The Holy Spirit won't make us do something that concerns our freewill. This means when we're doing something against God's ways, He will nudge us, make our hearts pound, and let us feel uncomfortable until we act in obedience. But it is our choice to act in obedience to Him. We cannot expect to say, "God, please let the Holy Spirit lead this conversation," and then speak and act however we want to. It is our choice to obey the Holy Spirit when He is correcting us from the inside. "Don't make God's Spirit sad. The Spirit makes sure that someday you will be free from your sins" (Ephesians 4:30 CEV).

It pleases God when we accept help from the Holy Spirit to be free from our sins, which include the sins that come from our mouth. He sent the Holy Spirit to help us. Let us receive His help! "But the Helper, the Holy Spirit, whom the Father will send in My name, He will teach you all things, and bring to your remembrance all that I said to you" (John 14:26 ESV). He does this all out of love for our spiritual growth. Embrace it! We have the power to stop dead in our tracks and obey.

What will the Holy Spirit do to try and get our attention?

_____

_____

Is it possible to stop what you're doing to obey the Holy Spirit?

_____

_____

How can you obey the Holy Spirit when He brings conviction?

_____

_____

There is "life and death in the tongue," which is why we must be careful with our words (Proverbs 18:21). "Your own soul is nourished when you are kind, but you destroy yourself when you are cruel" (Proverbs 11:17 NLT). The words that come from our mouth are either considered wise or foolish; they either help or hinder (Proverbs 11:9). Our words are always heard, whether they are heard from the natural world or supernatural realm; the tongue gives power to words which give power to those whose ears they land on. The power that words give will either be for the positive or for the negative in someone's life.

GOD-CENTERED FRIENDSHIPS

What could positive words do for someone in their life?

_____

_____

What could negative words do for someone in their life?

_____

_____

Who hears the words spoken from our mouths when no one is around?

_____

_____

Do you think our words could be used as ammo from the enemy as an attack on ourselves and the person we're talking about?

_____

_____

When we converse with others every single day, we can choose our conversation topics, how we handle our conversations, and how we glorify Jesus in the conversation; we can choose to be pleasing to God or not. When we surround ourselves with God minded friendships, it should help us get prepared for the relationships we have that include nonbelievers and believers alike. Christlike friends can help build us up if they want God to be the center of friendship talks.

With whom do you talk scripture?

_____

_____

Is scripture a part of your daily life or just on Sundays?

_____

_____

Life-giving words are positive and encouraging. Is it possible to control your tongue even in difficult situations? (See Proverbs 15:1.)

_____

_____

Praying for each other is one way to engage in scripture with God. Ask Him for the positive and encouraging words your friends need to hear right now.

Allow the leader of the small group to pray. Then this is a great time to share prayer requests. After prayer requests are shared, this is also a good time to share if God has been meeting the previous week's prayer requests of each member. Expressing His works is a great way for driving faith. If you don't see Him working yet for a specific prayer request, don't be afraid to start a discussion. Small groups are considered a "safe zone" that is condemnation-free.

Please remember that prayer requests are sacred and are not to be used as gossip outside the group. Respect each member of the small group and take to heart their needs for this week.

Week 6

What Brings You Together? Gossip or God?

It Is Possible to Tame Our Tongues with God's Grace

"Telling lies about others is as harmful as hitting them with an ax, wounding them with a sword, or shooting them with a sharp arrow" (Proverbs 25:18 NLT).

Let's get straight to the point: "Gossip is no good! It causes hard feelings and comes between friends" (Proverbs 16:28 CEV). King Solomon had much to say about gossip in the book of Proverbs. We'll be examining many of the gossip verses from Proverbs this week. Proverbs 16:28 clearly states what gossip can do to relationships. Because of what gossip can cause, we are to heed the careful and specific warning that "gossip is no good!"

But what is gossip exactly? Leviticus 19:16 NASB explains gossip as this, "You must not go about spreading slander among your people. You must not endanger the life of your neighbor. I am the Lord." We are told from this verse that gossip is spreading slander, misinformation, or information not for you to tell. The *Oxford Dictionary* describes *gossip* as "casual or unconstrained conversation or reports about other people, typically involving details that are not confirmed as being true" (1984). When we look at gossip from either the biblical or worldly perspective, the definition is close to the same.

This brings us to our first and foremost question: What brings your relationships together? Gossip or God? Do you get together or call each other specifically to gossip, or do you get together in a way that builds a solid friendship based on God's ways? This is your time to be honest and open in discussion with the group as this may remove possible blinders about some of your relationships.

"Where there is no fuel a fire goes out; where there is no gossip, arguments come to end. Troublemakers start trouble, just as sparks and fuel start a fire. There is nothing so delicious as the taste of gossip! It melts in your mouth" (Proverbs 26:20–22 CEV).

Think of the gossip process as a dinner party from start to finish. You get to the dinner party, and the hors d'oeuvres are gossip. The hors d'oeuvres look good, so you take one and then another. As Proverbs 26 describes, gossip tastes so good that you won't want to stop eating it. Then you move into the dinner, which will serve anger, pain, distrust, bitterness, and lies. Following dinner is dessert which will consist of wanting negative attention and a need to bring down reputations that once respected you. Once you're at the dinner party, it's hard to leave because of how good it can taste.

Gossip is fuel to get a blazing fire of trouble. We need to bridle our tongue to keep it from tasting the instant sinful gratification that gossip can cause in our mouths.

It's awful, but gossip runs rampant in the church. A little "church gossip" can easily turn into a blazing fire. Oftentimes, it sounds like this: "We need to pray for [name]. They're going through [gossip entered here as the information is spilled from mouth to any listening ears]. Only with the permission of the person should we share reasons why we need to pray for them. Otherwise, a simple "please put [name] on your prayer list" will suffice.

How can you put out the fire of gossip among your relationships?

GOD-CENTERED FRIENDSHIPS

Did you know that gossip can cause so many secondary sins?

_____

_____

How can you bridle your tongue and protect your ears (mind and soul) from gossip?

_____

_____

Tough bonus question: Do you control gossip that comes to you? Or does gossip control you?

_____

_____

Gossip is a tool used by the enemy. It is considered filth and senseless talk. It separates friendships, and it causes us to sin against God by creating additional sin in the way of anger, distrust, bitterness, and more.

We shouldn't want to fall into the enemy's trap of gossip because of the pain it creates—not only against someone else but also against our own heart. What we feed ourselves mentally will feed our souls. If we take in gossip, our mind and heart will become corrupt. It is said elegantly in Proverbs 18:20–21 CEV, "Make your words good—you will be glad you did. Words can bring death or life! Talk too much, and you will eat everything you say." We need to be careful with what we say and how much should be said.

One of the best sayings is, "Does it need to be said? Does it need to be said by me? Does it need to be said now" (Carmen Looney)?

We are responsible for all our words. If what we say does not benefit anyone, it probably isn't worth saying. Our words will be counted and judged when we get to heaven. Our tongues need to be controlled, not just for others but for ourselves too.

How can we see the enemy's trap of gossip before we're in the middle of it?

_____

_____

Why do you think our words will be counted and judged?

_____

_____

Try having an accountability partner this week to combat gossip. Help keep each other in check during your own conversations. Check in with each other throughout the week to see how other conversations went. Talk about how you can improve on getting rid of gossip.

We are asked in Psalm 15 who may stay in God's temple. Among the list of attributes, it states, "Only those who obey God and do as they should. They speak the truth and don't spread gossip; they treat others fairly and don't say cruel things" (Psalm 15:1–3 CEV). Controlling our tongues can be difficult, but it is part of the growing process as a born-again Christian.

By being "born-again" spiritually, we start over with a spiritual age. Fortunately, God knows this; and He offers forgiveness, redemption, and correction. He allows us to grow up just as our earthly parents did when we lived under their care. Only God makes no mistakes. When we listen more and talk less, He rewards us for being innocent (Psalm 18:24). How sweet the sound.

Discuss Psalm 15 in your group. Break down the verse, word by word. Don't be afraid to open up in conversation about how you could improve in this area. Remember, small group environments are a "safe zone" and a chance to offer support to each other.

God offers us forgiveness, redemption, and correction for our mistakes. If we are children of God, we are called to be Christlike (Ephesians 5:1). This leads to a very important question: Do you

GOD-CENTERED FRIENDSHIPS

offer forgiveness, redemption, and correction to those who have hurt through gossip?

_____

_____

We lead by example. What are some ways you can lead by example when it comes to gossip?

_____

_____

Praying for each other is one way to stand up against the enemy's schemes in gossip. Go to God first before going to friends with sensitive information.

Allow the leader of the small group to pray. Then this is a great time to share prayer requests. After prayer requests are shared, this is also a good time to share if God has been meeting the previous week's prayer requests of each member. Expressing His works is a great way for driving faith. If you don't see Him working yet for a specific prayer request, don't be afraid to start a discussion. Small groups are considered a "safe zone" that is condemnation-free.

Please remember that prayer requests are sacred and are not to be used as gossip outside the group. Respect each member of the small group and take to heart their needs for this week.

Week 7

I Have Your Back

Die to Ourselves. Love Others.

Offering help makes us too busy to criticize.

It's easy to be there for someone when times are good. But when someone needs extra support because things in life aren't going as they planned or hoped, is it still easy to offer support? A great friendship is having the support of a friend during good and bad times. I believe anyone can testify to this. We are all thankful for that friend that we can trust to lean on in every situation.

Love others as God loves you.

I am reminded of the story in the book of Luke of the man who was robbed and beaten and then left on the side of the road. Everyone who came across him went to the other side of the road because they didn't want to be bothered by his misfortune. One fellow did see him and offered a helping hand. I can only imagine how the poor injured man felt; his heart must have been delighted by the Good Samaritan! (Luke 10:25–37). What a friend both gained after that day.

Even though the Good Samaritan wasn't the man's friend yet, he had the compassionate heart of Christ. Many times, we find out quickly who is truly our friend. If we're doing good, our "friend" is jealous; if we're doing bad, then our "friend" isn't there supporting us. Let's be people of compassion with our current friends and friends-to-be.

GOD-CENTERED FRIENDSHIPS

How can you offer support to a friend during their good times?

_____

_____

How can you offer support to a friend during their bad times?

_____

_____

How can you offer support to someone you don't know, like the Good Samaritan?

_____

_____

Romans 12:10 CEV states, "Love each other as brothers and sisters and honor others more than you do yourself." When we love each other more than ourselves, it becomes easier to reach out that helping hand to the friend in distress. Our focus becomes about others in all situations, not just the easy moments for us. Even if we can't offer financial help or cook extra meals, we can share the godly love and wisdom when timing is right. "You obey the law of Christ when you offer each other a helping hand" (Galatians 6:2 CEV). We are called to offer ourselves to others.

Most of the time, we are all capable of offering some type of service to others. There are plenty of meals that don't cost a lot to offer someone who is going through hard times. Most of us can afford the time and the money to offer a ride. How about some extra cash, a gas station gift card, or groceries for someone?

Here is the story of the widow who gave all she had to show us how important Jesus thinks of this subject:

> Jesus sat down opposite the place where the offerings were put and watched the crowd putting their money into the temple treasury. Many

rich people threw in large amounts. But a poor widow came and put in two very small copper coins, worth only a few cents. Calling his disciples to him, Jesus said, "Truly I tell you, this poor widow has put more into the treasury than all the others. They all gave out of their wealth; but she, out of her poverty, put in everything—all she had to live on." (Mark 12:41–44 NIV)

What happens when we love others more than ourselves?

_____

_____

What would be examples of someone who could use a ready-made meal brought to them?

_____

_____

Based on the widow's story, what is important to Jesus regarding "giving"?

_____

_____

Much of scripture refers to helping others and then follows up with the reason, and the reason is love. Jesus loved us so much that He gave His life for us. What a friend is He! "Now I tell you to love each other as I have loved you. The greatest way to show love for friends is to die for them" (John 15:12–13 CEV). As Jesus acted out this verse in a physical way, thank goodness! I believe what God is saying to us for our daily relationships is to die to ourselves so we can offer ourselves to others, like Jesus did.

GOD-CENTERED FRIENDSHIPS

What are some ways that you can die to yourself today?

_____

_____

How has God blessed you?

_____

_____

We will be diving deeper in continued study of what healthy friendship boundaries are in series 2 of *God-Centered Friendships*. *Implement the study!*

Implement what you have learned from the study over the following week. Putting into practice what you've learned is a great way to fully understand how Jesus wants us to live. You can either do this by yourself and or do this with your small group!

Creating a gift basket for someone in need is a great way to get your entire small group involved. If you don't know anyone that could use some help, ask your church staff to lead you in the right direction. Gathering items for a homeless shelter or foster children is another great way to get your small group to come together for God's kingdom! Start a plan before dismissing the group!

"God works through us to reach others."

Praying for each other is one way to help. Petitioning for others to God means you care enough to bring their needs in front of the throne. Even when everything is going great, strength and courage in the Lord will sustain us and keep us humbled as we depend on Him.

Allow the leader of the small group to pray. Then this is a great time to share prayer requests. After prayer requests are shared, this is also a good time to share if God has been meeting the previous week's prayer requests of each member. Expressing His works is a great way for driving faith. If you don't see Him working yet for a specific prayer request, don't be afraid to start a discussion. Small groups are considered a "safe zone" that is condemnation-free.

SIERRA DERBY

Please remember that prayer requests are sacred and are not to be used as gossip outside the group. Respect each member of the small group and take to heart their needs for this week.

Week 8

Love Trumps Worldly Feelings

Love, Love, Love

"Honor God by accepting each other, as Christ has accepted you" (Romans 15:7 CEV).

God makes it a point to talk about love throughout the Bible because that's *who* He is. He is *love* (1 John 4:8). He is not worldly; He cannot be worldly because *worldly* is another word for *sinful*. It is impossible for God to be anything other than *holy*.

We, on the other hand, can be worldly because we chose sin from the serpent. When sin was presented to mankind, we took it and sinned against the Holy One by disobeying Him and dishonoring our position under Him. Although we bear the weight of sin, Jesus came and gave us the opportunity for renewal in the name of the Lord. Now we are called to be in this world and not of this world (John 17:14–15).

Why can God not sin?

_____

_____

How did sin affect us?

_____

_____

Can we love like God loves?

_____

_____

"The gospel is more effective with our actions."

We have a great mission in this life. God entrusts us with the purpose of bringing more people to know Him from the world. How do we do this? We let His love shine through us instead of our emotions or worldly feelings. We can make this task of overcoming our feelings easier by having an accountability partner—a friend to be exact. A trusted friend can help call us out when we let our emotions get a little out of control. Jesus showed us that He had emotions, too, but He controlled His emotions; they didn't control Him.

His love overpowered everything, so He acted godly in every circumstance. Since He was God in the flesh, I like to think He was His own accountability partner. However, to be our example, He always turned to the Father and prayed. He showed us how to depend on God to be His accountability partner, His trusted and forever friend. We, on the other hand, need more help than ourselves; we need Jesus. A trusted Christian friend always helps too.

Do you let your emotions control you?

_____

_____

What are the trigger points when you feel like you can't control your emotions?

_____

_____

GOD-CENTERED FRIENDSHIPS

Does God's love overpower every flesh feeling to come over us?

_____

_____

How do we "get" God's love in us?

_____

_____

Psalm 1:1–2 CEV says, "God blesses those people who refuse evil advice or join in sneering at God. Instead, the law of the Lord makes them happy, and they think about it day and night." All of Psalm 1 helps us to understand what it is like for people who chase after God's way, or the world's way. Christlike friendships allow us to give and receive God's wisdom and helps us refuse evil advice.

When sin entered the world through Satan's deception, it entered us when we were born. God says it doesn't have to end there. God said, "We are created in His image" (Genesis 1:27). Psalm 1 tells us not to join in the evil ways of the world. This means we can control our emotions and be set apart from our sinful identity. A friend should love us for us, just as Christ does, but friends should want to help us grow the way God wants us to grow. He created us to be something entirely different than what the world says we are to be. He created us to have a purpose in His kingdom on earth and in heaven (Romans 8:28).

Allowing our emotions to run rampant stunts our growth and friends should lovingly point out when we let the world get the best of us. If we allow Him to guide us and if we follow His ways, He will transform us into His vision of who we are. He will transform our wicked hearts into loving hearts. We will always be able to love like Him. God's love is overflowing and ready for us to live by. Spreading the love of God is the only way to overcome ourselves and to show Him to others.

Read over Psalm 1. Follow the reading with a group discussion.

Is God's love more powerful than anything on earth?

_____

_____

Praying for each other is one way to overcome worldly feelings. Sometimes, it doesn't seem possible to love like God, but with prayer, it is possible!

Allow the leader of the small group to pray. Then this is a great time to share prayer requests. After prayer requests are shared, this is also a good time to share if God has been meeting the previous week's prayer requests of each member. Expressing His works is a great way for driving faith. If you don't see Him working yet for a specific prayer request, don't be afraid to start a discussion. Small groups are considered a "safe zone" that is condemnation-free.

Please remember that prayer requests are sacred and are not to be used as gossip outside the group. Respect each member of the small group and take to heart their needs for this week.

Additional Note Space

Use this space for additional note taking throughout your group sessions

SIERRA DERBY

Prayer Requests

God calls us to petition in prayer not only for ourselves but also for others! Praying for each other is one the best things you can do in your new friendship!

Follow up with concern for another's prayer request during the week. It will mean so much to them!

Please remember that prayer requests are sacred and are not to be used as gossip outside the group. Respect each member of the small group and take to heart their needs for this week.

You might be surprised how praying for someone else can help them *and* how God will also use it to grow you too.

Use the space below to record the prayer request and date for each person.

Date	Name	Prayer Request	Answered

SIERRA DERBY

Date	Name	Prayer Request	Answered

Leading Your Group

"They broke bread together in different homes and shared their food happily and freely, while praising God. Everyone liked them, and each day the Lord added to their group others who were being saved" (Acts 2:46–47 CEV).

The following is an example for a two-hour small group gathering. You can follow each step of this outline, but please find what works best for your group.

Tips for your small group:

- *Pray, pray, pray!* Don't forget to begin and end the group in prayer each week asking God to direct the group and open everyone's hearts to the study.
- I find it best for each member to bring a contributing dish to pass each week, whether you decide to do dinner or snacks.
- Assigning accountability partners allows your group members to stay focused throughout the week, as well as create friendships.
- The first week of small group is a great time to get know to each other through open discussion and to talk about what each person is hoping to get out of this study over the next nine weeks (eight weeks if you jump right into the study in week one).
- Allow each person to contribute discussion for answering questions. You may want to lead in the prequestion reading, or you may want others to take turns in paragraph reading.

Remember, you are not a teacher as a small group leader. However, you are a kingdom host willing to open your home for others to gather in His name. The following paragraphs for leading a group is stated from Chip Ingram in *The Invisible War*. I think he explains the small group leader role perfectly.

Focus on Facilitating, Not Teaching: Your expertise is needed in facilitating the teaching and cultivating good conversation during the discussion time.

Be Yourself: The others in your group will appreciate and follow your example of openness and honesty as you lead—so set a good example! The best way to encourage those in your group is not to impress them with your own wisdom, but with your sincere desire to live out these principles in your own life. When they sense that you are "real"—that you are not "above" the issues that challenge them—they will be encouraged to press in and press on.

Be Prepared: Review the study before your group meets each week. Focus can be lost during discussion time as people present opinions that may detract from the focus of the lesson or may not represent Biblical teaching. Keep things on track by pointing the conversation back to the material.

Have fun in your group!

About the Author

Sierra Derby is the founder of One Ministries Global, a growing international ministry that is devoted to helping people understand who God created them to be and how they can accomplish being their best person in the name of Christ.

Sierra and her husband, Brent, also own a yacht renovation company, Wood Line Productions, where they work all over the United States renovating boats of all sizes inside and out.

Together, they don't have any human children, but they do share their home with two amazingly lovable pups, Porter, a bullmastiff, and Samson, a Staffordshire terrier. Both were rescued and have been renewed!

Sierra grew up as a Michigander, born a Coloradoan, and made a pit stop in Nevada for a while before settling in Georgia with her husband and fur babies. She's full of courage and loves growing in the Lord.

CPSIA information can be obtained
at www.ICGtesting.com
Printed in the USA
LVHW031333040821
694432LV00006B/960